I Own My Magic

SELF-TALK FOR BLACK WOMEN
AFFIRMATIONS FOR SELF-CARE AND EMPOWERMENT

G. MICHELLE GOODLOE, LCSW

This book is dedicated to my mom, Gennifer.

— ❖ —

Published by:
Ulysses Press
PO Box 3440
Berkeley, CA 94703
www.ulyssespress.com

ISBN: 978-1-64604-327-9
Library of Congress Control Number: 2021945955

Printed in the United States by Versa Press
10 9 8 7 6 5 4 3 2 1

Acquisitions editor: Ashten Evans
Managing editor: Claire Chun
Project manager: Tyanni Niles
Editor: Michele Anderson
Proofreader: Renee Rutledge
Front cover design: Aderice Palmer-Jones
Interior design and layout: Jake Flaherty

NOTE TO READERS: This book has been written and published for informational and educational purposes only. It is not intended to serve as medical advice or to be any form of medical treatment. You should always consult with your physician before altering or changing any aspect of your medical treatment. Do not stop or change any prescription medications without the guidance and advice of your physician. Any use of the information in this book is made on the reader's good judgment and is the reader's sole responsibility. This book is not intended to diagnose or treat any medical condition and is not a substitute for a physician.

Contents

Message to the Reader

Hey there,

I can't tell you how excited I am for you to dive into this journal. There may be several reasons why you've decided to take the time to immerse yourself in this text. You could be looking for a place to express yourself or exploring ways to feel encouraged. Be affirmed that this journal was created with you, your experiences, and your heart in mind.

Black women are *incredible* people. We hold a variety of roles that help this world go 'round and have persevered through the most challenging, difficult, and complicated situations imaginable. For generations, Black women have been expected to be strong—for themselves and for others—and in this journal, I want to give you permission to feel *soft*. This journal invites you to gently put down the burdens, hardships, and adversities that you have been carrying, and to be and feel *seen*.

And how magical it is to be and feel *seen*.

It feels like most of my life has been dedicated to feeling seen—to getting to that place where I was visible, appreciated, and . . . worthy. As a Black female social worker, I felt defined by my roles and that my identity was wrapped up in being "strong." This narrative included working as hard as I could and feeling the pressure to *earn* the right to be seen.

It wasn't until a few months into my first full-time job that another woman who looked like me saw the Black Superwoman cape that I was wearing. I was sitting in a weekly one-on-one meeting to discuss my job and my tasks with my supervisor, a trauma-informed and clinically licensed counselor. As usual, I came prepared and eager, with a notebook full of notes and a smile plastered on my face. I was ready to *perform*, ready to earn the visibility I desperately desired.

She sat across from me, her face relaxed and her body rested—so opposite of my own, as I sat upright, with my body on the edge of my seat, notes stacked perfectly on my lap, and sweat rolling down my back.

She leaned in toward me, with her brow furrowed, and calmly asked, "Are you *always* this way?"

My body froze.

I Own My Magic

I quickly responded, "*This* way? What do you mean?"

I remember holding my breath, now terrified of where this conversation was going.

"Yes, *this* way," she continued. "Always smiling, always ready. Do you know it's OK to just *be* here?" She smiled gently and reached for my hand.

As soon as I felt her physical touch, the tears welled in my eyes and streamed down my face. Never, and especially never in any professional environment, had I been given permission to just *be*.

And that feeling of being seen shook me to my core. As I laid my defenses down on her office floor, my body went from tense to soft, my heart open and feeling safe. My breath regulated and slowed down.

I couldn't even believe how much I was holding, how much effort I was exerting to feel seen, how exhausted I was to rest from performing.

This woman, an African woman who came to the United States to continue her incredible healing work with people impacted by interpersonal violence, took the time to *see me*. In her genuine care, she created space for me to feel seen. Her kindness gave me permission to own my magic, without having to earn it, work for it, or perform for it.

I worked with this wonderful human being for some years and have always felt a tremendous amount of gratitude for the space she provided for me. This experience is one of a select few that led you and me to connect through this text today.

You too deserve to feel *seen*.

You too deserve space to feel *soft*.

You too deserve permission to just *be*.

You too deserve to own your magic.

My hope is that this journal offers you a chance to breathe too.

Black women can be each other's greatest supporters. We can be each other's nurturers, teachers, cheerleaders, and advisers. Know that you are among a powerful community of sensational women, and all of us deserve to exhale together.

There is a good chance that some of the questions and prompts that you discover in this journal will be familiar to you, while others may be brand-new questions that no one has asked you before. This journal is centered on exploring some of the parts of you that may have been guarded or protected for a long time. Please, take your time with these discoveries. There is no rush in how you self-reflect.

There are several entries, journal prompts, and affirmations sprinkled throughout this book for you to take in. Some of the answers to the prompts may come to you naturally, while others may require you to pause, reflect, and think. There is no right or wrong way to use this journal—you get to choose how you own your magic.

How to Use This Journal

Consider the following ideas to create your own self-care practice using this journal:

▶ Decide on and dedicate a time of day for you to reflect alone. Are you a morning person? Or do you favor the evenings? Are your lunch breaks your favorite time to have to yourself? Or is right after breakfast a good time to self-reflect? Choose a time that works for you to consistently use this journal.

The best time for me to use this journal is:

_____

▶ Do what feels right for you to flow through each question, prompt, and affirmation. To create some structure around how you reflect, you may want to reflect with one prompt at a time or carve out some time to sit and explore each section. You get to decide what works best for you.

I want to explore this journal by:

_____

_____

_____

▶ Choose which comforts help you self-reflect. Do you like to curl up on a spot on the couch? Or do you like to sit upright at a table? Does silence help you to reflect? Or do you enjoy some music in the background? See what feels right for you when setting up your space.

This is how I'd like to set up my space to self-reflect:

_____

_____

_____

▶ Pause and reflect on what comes up for you as you read this journal. Keep your favorite writing utensil handy to write, draw, or list the ideas, thoughts, feelings, and reactions that you notice.

▶ I encourage you to read aloud the different affirmations and quotes that are sprinkled throughout this journal. There is something special about hearing yourself state affirming, encouraging phrases. That's part of your self-talk!

▶ Try your best. It's OK if you do not have every answer to every question in this guide. Try your absolute best to explore your habits, routines, and mindset around rest and self-care.

I will try my best to own my magic through this journal by:

_____

_____

_____

▶ Choose to let go of perfectionist thoughts. There is no such thing as a "perfect answer" to the prompts and questions that come up in this guide. You may feel stuck or challenged at times, and that's OK. You are taking new steps to do what's best for you. Know that it's acceptable to make mistakes and not always get it right. You always have a chance to start again.

CHAPTER 1

Self-Care, Selfishness, and Self-Worth

What exactly is "self-talk"?

Self-talk is the encouragement and support you communicate to yourself and with yourself. While you will find excerpts, information, and ideas to help you practice self-talk, this journal supports you in creating your own encouraging ways to connect to how you communicate with yourself.

What exactly is "self-care"?

Self-care is the practice of routinely identifying and addressing what you need to show up as your favorite version of yourself. Self-care is a combination of habits, practices, rituals, and routines that you put energy into to take care of yourself the best way you know how.

 SELF-REFLECT

How do you feel about creating space for your self-talk and self-care?

_____

_____

_____

Have you ever felt like taking time for yourself was . . .
selfish?

_____

_____

_____

If this feels true for you, I invite you to think back to where
you first learned this. Using the prompts below, reflect on
your feelings about taking care of you.

When did you first identify self-care as being selfish? Do
you remember who told you?

_____

_____

_____

What did they say that resonated with you?

_____

_____

_____

❖

On my own self-care journey, I first saw my self-care as selfishness as an undergraduate in college. My friends described me as a "busybody," and they couldn't have been more right.

As a busybody, I had my hands in a little bit of everything. I joined a few clubs, participated in some activities, and had a full course load, semester after semester. I found instant gratification in socializing with my peers without the hover of parental supervision. Being in college was freeing. I relished not having a curfew and felt a sense of power and control in *finally* being able to make my own decisions.

But all this freedom was unfamiliar to me. In many instances, it was overwhelming, and I wanted to take full advantage of this freedom I was given. I remember learning early on that you have time for only two out of three things in college: time to sleep, time to study, and time to have a social life. Let's just say for my first few years of college, I didn't get much sleep.

If I wasn't hopping from class to class, I was front and center at a meeting or doing the most at a party. My social life was full and all-consuming. I remember feeling both excited and stressed most of the time. And at times I found myself wondering, "Am I *even* doing enough?"

Because more than anything, I wanted to feel important and *seen*.

I wanted to be wanted. I wanted the people around me to know that they were important to me and that I was dependable. I wanted them to know I was the one to be trusted and I wanted to *earn* their love. With this mindset, I started focusing less on school and more on being the fun-loving friend. My grades began to suffer and the expectations I set for my social life became more and more important to me. My priorities shifted, and my self-worth became tied to how much I *did*. I tried to find my self-worth through others' expectations of me and what I could do for *them*.

As with so many college students in the millennial age, the ways that I cared for myself included running through the campus as exercise and fueling my body with junk food and portable caffeine-ridden drinks. I was constantly scrolling through social media and texting away on my phone, responding to messages and spreading myself too thin.

I would sign up to host this and volunteer to create that. My social life went from existing only on the weekends to bleeding into my weeknights and even my weekdays. By my junior year, I was the college version of burned out. My social life was now my priority, and my academic career was suffering because of it. And *sleep*? What sleep?

The summer before my senior year, I chose event planning and parties over classes one too many times. I failed one of the core classes I needed to graduate, and my grade point average dipped lower than I had ever seen it dip before. This was devastating, as I had made the conscious choice to not prioritize my own studies—all because I did not want to appear *selfish*. And because of this choice, that summer and the remainder of my college career were dedicated to repairing all the damage that I had done.

There is a big difference between taking care of yourself and being selfish. A selfish person prioritizes their needs, and their needs alone. By definition, "selfishness" means to see only oneself, one's needs, and one's wants without recognizing that others also exist in spaces to have their needs and wants met. For someone to be considered selfish, they usually act:

- Uncaring of others
- Incapable or unwilling to recognize the needs of others
- Reliant on blaming and shaming to get what they want
- Trying to get what they want by any means necessary or at the cost of another's needs

Many Black women are taught that prioritizing your needs is an act rooted in being uncaring of others. Many people from Black communities and other communities of color view self-care for women as not caring for your family, being neglectful of your loved ones, not living up to your womanly duties, and selfishly focusing on yourself. This was the message that I learned. And this message carried weight into my young adult life. There are social, generational, gender-based, and cultural implications that tie selfishness and practicing self-care together.

The reality is that self-care is *not* selfish.

In choosing to take care of your needs, you are creating space to show up as your favorite version of yourself—the version that you feel the proudest of and the most excited about. When you are functioning as your healthiest, most energetic, and most vibrant self, the benefits are *abundant*. Your self-care can help you become more focused on what is important to you, more intentional in your relationships, and more skillful in the areas of your life that you care about.

Though I have a great deal of compassion and understanding for who I was when I was younger, I could have used some support in understanding how to determine my own self-worth. In focusing so much on pleasing others, I had no room to reflect on how I felt about *me*. I needed to be told that saying no and spending time on what was important to me weren't selfish at all. Self-worth through practicing self-care is acknowledging your *own* needs and creating time, space, and energy to take care of those needs. Appreciating your self-worth includes understanding that you are important—that there is space for you to take care of yourself well.

It is difficult to discover and appreciate your worth if you are distracted and pressured to please others. Taking care of your needs does not mean you do not care for others. Caring for yourself can actually help strengthen your capacity to care for others and put energy into what's important to you. Practicing self-care and knowing your self-worth are all about getting grounded and affirmed in loving who you are and setting boundaries around how you can preserve this self-love.

SELF CHECK-IN: SELF-CARE, SELFISHNESS, AND SELF-WORTH

What would you like to unlearn about self-care being selfish?

_____

_____

_____

What message would you like to create for yourself to continue practicing self-care?

_____

_____

_____

What is one step you would like to take to start taking care of yourself better?

_____

_____

_____

—————— ❖ ——————

Affirmation

I am not selfish for taking care of myself.
I am worth taking care of myself.

CHAPTER 2

Caring for Your Health

There's no doubt that your health is a top priority when it comes to your self-care.

Your health is a foundational part of you and has a heavy hand in determining how you function, how you show up, and how you are able to engage in your daily life. In your experience as a Black woman, your risk of experiencing challenges with your physical and mental health is *great*. You need your health and your energy to do the many things that are important to you. When you think of your health, think of your physical, mental, and spiritual well-being.

Taking care of your body can mean *many* different things. From breaking a sweat while working out to taking time to get your hair done, physical self-care includes taking care of *all* the physical parts of your body. And as a Black woman, it means holding space for the intricate ways that you care for your precious body.

Affirmation

Today, I will take steps to prepare myself for the good, healthy, and abundant changes that are coming my way.

ACTIVITY: BODY SCAN

Take a moment to reflect on what your body, mind, and spirit need, starting with this physical well-being activity.

1. Find a comfortable place to lie down on your back, close your eyes, and take a deep breath.

2. Starting with your toes, slowly recognize each part of your body. Gently "scan" your body by checking in on how each of your body parts feel. This reflection may take a few minutes, so give yourself some time. Once you have completed your body scan, reflect on the questions below.

Using the image at right, circle the areas of your body that you noticed felt tense or stressed, or in pain. Describe how these body parts are feeling today.

_____

_____

_____

_____

Which parts of your body need extra support and care today?

_____

_____

Are there any parts of your body that have needed additional care for a while? If so, which ones?

_____

How would you like to take care of these parts of your body today?

_____

_____

How are you feeling about your body today?

_____

_____

Which parts of your body feel well and healthy today?

_____

_____

How do you want to appreciate these parts of your body today?

_____

_____

Name four of your favorite ways to take care of your body:

1. _____

   _____

2. _____

   _____

3. _____

   _____

4. _____

   _____

Which part of your body feels the most well and maintained? How are you currently taking care of this part of you?

_____

_____

Which part of your body needs the most attention right now? How would you like to take care of this part of you?

_____

_____

———————— ❖ ————————

My hair is a significant part of my body.

Like so many of us as young girls, I had my hair chemically "relaxed." With tight, coiled curls blooming out of my scalp, my hair was so different from my mother's long, wavy locks. As I was growing up, my mom tried her best to take care of my hair with the help of a local Midwestern salon. Every four to six weeks, I dreaded spending an entire Saturday stiffly seated in a busy salon, feeling the sting of the relaxer and the heat of the flat iron that stretched my natural curls into straight tresses.

After almost two decades of monthly perms, I remember sitting in a salon in my early twenties and waiting for a new-to-me stylist to take me through the fiery process of chemically straightening my hair. It was summertime, and I was hot, tired, frustrated, and stressed about spending the little bit of money I had on this ongoing hair-care service. But going to the salon was a reflex for me—I never thought twice about these monthly visits to get my hair done, and until this point in my life, I had never considered wearing and caring for my hair in any other way. It was what I thought I was *supposed* to do to take care of this part of my body.

This stylist, who I found on Google only hours before my appointment, had overbooked herself. Just like I would as a little girl, I was sitting and waiting to get my hair done for most of my precious Saturday. It was that very day, in August 2011, that I decided that this would be my *last* perm appointment for no other reason than I wanted my Saturdays back. I was ready for something new and eager to break my dependence on the hair salon.

That day, I began my natural hair journey. And I haven't looked back since.

SELF-REFLECT

A Black woman's hair is a precious part of her body. Our hair, with its texture, colors, styles, and versatility, is often a special part of who we are. Our hair is influential and magnificent, no matter how we choose to wear it. Take a moment to reflect on your own experiences with your hair.

Describe your hair when you were growing up. How did you feel about your hair as a young girl?

Who helped take care of your hair when you were a little girl? What would they do to take care of it?

How do you feel about your hair in its current state?

What about your hair brings you joy?

_____

_____

What about your hair feels challenging?

_____

_____

What has been your favorite hairstyle, cut, or color? What did you love about this style?

_____

_____

Which hairstyle would you not repeat? How come?

_____

_____

Are there any hairstyles that you would never try? Which ones?

_____

_____

What hairstyle have you been dying to try? What's holding you back from trying it?

❖

Affirmation

My mistakes, my flaws, and my imperfections do not and will not define who I am.

Your mental health is a part of you that needs care, energy, and attention.

When we say "mental well-being," we are looking into taking care of our thoughts, feelings, and reactions. There are many stigmas attached to addressing mental health—stigmas like if you choose to take care of your mental health, your sanity is in question. Some people believe that mental-health care is equivalent to being weak or that caring for your mental health makes you inferior.

These stigmas are unjustified but powerful within the Black community. Similarly, some of these stigmas surrounding mental health are derived from the discriminatory and unjust treatment of Black people. It is important to recognize and hold space for this complicated social construction of health, because you deserve to have knowledge about what the barriers are to this care so you have the opportunity to address *all* parts of your health.

Caring for your mental health means nurturing the types of thoughts you have, recognizing your feelings, and learning your reactions. From mindfulness practices to going to therapy, there are ways to take care of this part of you.

 SELF-REFLECT

When reflecting on your mental health and the stigmas that can be attached, ask yourself:

What were you taught about your mental health?

_____

_____

What did you learn about mental health later in your life?

_____

_____

What about your mental health do you wish you learned earlier in your life?

_____

_____

What were some stereotypes, misconceptions, or stigmas that you learned about mental health as a Black woman? What was told to you?

_____

_____

What did you learn from the media or in school about Black women's mental health that stuck with you? What do you remember?

_____

_____

❖

We all experience many different emotions. And for many Black women, it can be difficult, and even scary, to acknowledge and create space for the different emotions that we have.

Some of our emotions can feel heavy and some of our emotions can feel light. Our emotions remind us that we care about things and that we are alive. Our emotions remind us of our *humanity*. Let's spend some time recognizing the different heavy and light emotions that you may be feeling.

ACTIVITY: RECOGNIZING YOUR HEAVY AND LIGHT EMOTIONS

Which heavy emotions have you been feeling lately? Heavy emotions are just that—weighted feelings that are sometimes hard to recognize, hard to sit with, and hard to process.

There are a lot of heavy feelings here, so take your time. Circle the emotions below that resonate with you the most:

Afraid	Frustrated	Overwhelmed
Angry	Grief stricken	Preoccupied
Annoyed	Heartbroken	Sad
Anxious	Hopeless	Tired
Betrayed	Hurt	Unhappy
Confused	Irritated	Unsafe
Disappointed	Lonely	Vengeful
Disgusted	Numb	Worried

I Own My Magic

Which heavy emotions resonated the most with you?
What came up for you when recognizing these emotions?

If this applies, which heavy feelings were you not "allowed"
to feel when you were younger? Which heavy feelings
were minimized, ignored, or denied to you?

Which heavy feelings are difficult for you to recognize?
What about these feelings is difficult to recognize?

Our light emotions can leave us feeling light and weightless.
These emotions can feel good, warm, and special to us.
Sometimes we even chase after these feelings to avoid the
heavy ones.

Which light emotions have you been feeling lately? Circle the emotions below that resonate with you the most:

Appreciated	Grounded	Proud
Comforted	Honored	Relaxed
Compassionate	Hopeful	Relieved
Determined	Joyful	Respected
Energetic	Organized	Safe
Excited	Peaceful	Understood
Focused	Prepared	Validated
Grateful	Protected	Well rested

Which light emotions resonated the most with you? What came up for you when recognizing these emotions?

_____

_____

If this applies, which light feelings were you not "allowed" to feel when you were younger? Which light feelings were minimized, ignored, or denied to you?

_____

I Own My Magic

Which light feelings are difficult for you to recognize?
What about these feelings is difficult to recognize?

One way to take care of your mental well-being is not only to recognize your heavy and light feelings but to create practices that help you take care of yourself when you feel these different emotions.

What is one way that you would like to take care of yourself when you are feeling a heavy emotion?

What is one way that you would like to cherish your light emotions?

———— ❖ ————

Ways to sit with heavy feelings:

▶ Recognize the heavy feelings in your body. How is your body handling these feelings? Identify what your body needs to feel better.

▶ Process and safely release difficult and heavy feelings through journaling, venting, talking, or engaging in a self-care practice that is helpful to you.

Decide what feels right for you when you notice a heavy feeling.

▶ Do you need rest?

▶ Do you need to set or maintain a boundary?

▶ Do you need to engage in activism?

▶ Do you need support from others?

▶ Do you need more space and time to process?

The first time I experienced a panic attack, I didn't know it but learned to identify it later. I was scared and unfamiliar with what to do. After a couple of Google searches, I decided to try therapy after the panic attack to learn what was going on with me. The first time I saw a therapist, I was in my mid-twenties.

From the lengthy intake assessment to nervously sitting in the waiting room, I remember feeling judged and afraid of what to expect on the day of my first session. When I was called into the therapist's office, I sat uncomfortably in my seat, prepared to answer questions about what brought me into this dimly lit, essential-oil-smelling space.

The therapist sat across from me with her legs crossed and clipboard in hand. I remember her warm smile as she asked me what brought me in today. I envied her cool calmness as I tried to concisely explain how I experienced my panic attack. After she put down her clipboard and we began talking more casually about what I was going through, I eased back into the couch and shared how frightened I was to feel my body go into such an anxiety-ridden shock.

This therapist was the first of a few for me, as it took some time to find a mental health professional whom I felt comfortable with, understood what I was going through, and was able to offer me the support that I needed to feel safe in my own body. Mental health care can be a sensitive process. It may take some trial and error to discover the help, services, and support that you need to feel mentally and emotionally well.

 **SELF-REFLECT**

Take a moment to reflect on how you feel about seeking professional mental health care.

How do you feel about therapy? What do you know about it?

_____

_____

_____

Have you had a therapy session before? What do you remember about it?

_____

_____

_____

If you have experienced therapy before, what about it was helpful to you? What about your experience was not helpful?

_____

_____

_____

If you have not gone to therapy before, what questions do you have about it?

_____

_____

_____

——————— ❖ ———————

Things to consider when deciding to begin therapy:

▶ Think about why you are choosing to go into therapy. What do you need help with? What are you hoping to learn about yourself, your experiences, or both?

▶ What type of therapist are you looking for? Are you looking for a specialist in relationships, or someone who is trained in working with people who survived trauma?

Brainstorm what your needs are around therapeutic care.

▸ If the therapist offers a phone consultation, prepare a few questions to ask about their therapeutic style and if they help people who specialize in what you are hoping to heal from.

▸ Know that it's OK if you do not feel a connection to the therapist during the first session. You have the option to explore other therapists until you find the right fit for you.

Affirmation

All the good decisions that I'm making are adding up. Today I choose to keep going.

Your spiritual well-being is another special part of your health. Your spiritual identity, your feelings about your spirituality, and your spiritual practices are all parts of how you take care of your spiritual well-being.

As a Black woman, you may have many feelings about what spirituality means to you. Some thoughts about spirituality could revolve around experiences within religious organizations, places of worship, churches, synagogues, or temples. Other thoughts could be about energy, healing, connection, and mindfulness. Spirituality, as faith or organized religion, can bring about memories that are light, heavy, or a mix of both. As we recognize spirituality in this journal, we recognize that it is a unique experience rather than a singular one.

 **SELF-REFLECT**

Reflect on what you need for your spiritual well-being below.

How would you describe your spiritual identity? What does spirituality mean to you?

_____

_____

What do you need to feel spiritually well? Which practices, traditions, and communities support your spiritual well-being?

_____

_____

Do heavy emotions come up for you around spirituality, faith, or religion? If so, which heavy emotions are you noticing right now?

_____

_____

To feel spiritually well, think of three practices that help you take care of your spiritual well-being:

1. _____

2. _____

3. _____

How do you want your spirituality to help you feel?

_____

_____

——————— ❖ ———————

SELF CHECK-IN: CARING FOR YOUR HEALTH

What did you learn about yourself in this section?

What are you in the process of unlearning?

How do you want to take care of your physical health?

How would you like to take care of your mental health?

How would you like to take care of your spiritual health?

—————— ❖ ——————

Affirmation

Choosing to let go of what's no longer valuable to me gives me space, time, and energy to focus on what is.

CHAPTER 3

Releasing Your Superwoman Cape

How do you feel about "doing it all"?

Black women are sometimes seen as "Superwomen"—beings who are expected to do *all* things to perfection without breaking a sweat, complaining, or needing to rest. Let us not forget: Superheroes are *fictional* characters. This expectation to be Black Superwomen is actually and completely *unrealistic*.

Black Superwomen are expected to passionately fulfill every role in their life, show up for others fully, and do it all while remaining "strong." This "heroic" title often comes with an immense amount of societal, cultural, professional, and personal pressure. And this pressure can feel *exhausting*.

Black Superwomanhood often leaves little room for us to feel our humanity and to just *be*. The expectations are oftentimes idealistic, at best, and the consequences of constantly being pressured to fulfill this role are monumental. There was a reason why my former supervisor's gentle recognition of my humanness was such a powerful moment for me, because up until then, I felt pressured to fulfill the role of a Black Superwoman. And Black Superwomen are expected to do things that a typical human being isn't expected to do.

 **SELF-REFLECT**

Take a moment to reflect on how you may have been feeling the pressure of Black Superwomanhood.

When and where did you first learn about the term "Black Superwoman"? How did it make you feel?

_____

_____

How do you feel when you are told that you are "strong"? What does "being strong" mean to you?

_____

_____

Sometimes society equates Black Superwomanhood with being "successful"—personally, professionally, or both. How do you feel about Black Superwomanhood and success?

_____

_____

Create your own vision of "success." In the space provided, draw images, use colors, and write the words that come to mind when you think of being successful:

Describe the last time you did not feel strong. What was happening around you? What were you feeling instead?

_____

_____

_____

_____

———————————— ❖ ————————————

ACTIVITY: THE ROLES THAT YOU HOLD

Take a moment to recognize some of the pressure you feel to do it all. What's been sitting on your shoulders lately? List these roles here:

_____

_____

_____

_____

What are the roles that you fulfill in your daily life? List the names of these roles and some of the responsibilities you have in them:

_____

_____

_____

_____

Which roles require most of your energy? How come?

_____

_____

_____

_____

Which roles feel most fulfilling? What about them fills you up?

_____

_____

_____

_____

Which roles feel the most draining for you?

_____

_____

_____

Is there anything you would change about the roles that
you hold right now in your life? If so, what would you
change? If not, how come?

_____

_____

_____

———————————— ❖ ————————————

Some of us did not volunteer for the roles that we hold.
Many Black women are expected to fulfill tasks and responsibilities because of cultural, societal, familial, or historical
expectations that have been passed down from Black
woman to Black woman, generation after generation. The
Black Superwoman is expected to fulfill these roles many

times over and continue the cycle of doing more, and more, and more.

Affirmation

Just because I can do it all doesn't mean I have to do it all.

One way to release some of the intense pressure that the Black Superwoman role holds is by creating, setting, and maintaining your boundaries.

Boundaries are the limits and expectations we create to keep ourselves feeling safe and balanced. We create boundaries in our relationships with others and our relationship with ourselves in an effort to protect our time, energy, space, and personal well-being.

Imagine: if your self-care is a body, your boundaries are the clothes it wears to protect it from the elements. Like a necessary shield, our boundaries form a protective barrier around us. It goes without saying that creating and maintaining boundaries is a necessary component to feeling physically, mentally, and spiritually balanced.

As a Black woman first entering the professional world, I experienced a bold introduction to creating boundaries. In graduate school, I was a counseling intern sharing an open office space with several other interns. The office space was busy, noisy, and bustling with people walking, talking, and working. In this setting, if I wasn't meeting with a client for counseling, oftentimes I was processing paperwork, organizing resources, and completing administrative tasks.

Like most working people, I regularly needed peace and quiet to complete my work. And as an intern, peace and quiet weren't just hard to come by—they were luxuries. I tried using my earphones to block out some of the noise and even tried to find a less busy time to process paperwork. Unfortunately, I was frequently interrupted by a coworker or a fellow intern with questions, requests, and conversation. I was frustrated—these distractions made it difficult to get my job done. And without the privilege of a door to close, it was difficult for me to set boundaries.

So I came up with an idea—I would create a sign.

I grabbed a couple of art supplies to create a sign that said:

"Currently typing away! Thank you for coming back later!"

The sign was created on printed paper and hung loosely by colorful yarn in between two of the intern desktop computers, in front of our office desks. The other interns thought this was *genius*. Finally, I would have a chance to set boundaries with the limited resources that I had.

Unfortunately for me, this well-intentioned gesture of setting limits did not sit well with one of the directors of the organization. While giving a tour of the space, this director pulled at the sign I crafted and huffed. She was a White woman in her late fifties with *significant* power at the organization. She intimidated me with her tall stature and in-your-face persona. While pulling at this sign, she exclaimed, "What is *this*? Did you receive *approval* from your supervisor to create this?"

My heart skipped a beat and sweat formed at the edge of my forehead. I felt embarrassed. Her calling me out, in front of my peers and her guests, was distressing, to say the least. My seemingly innocent act of creating some sense of privacy to complete my work was being *publicly shamed*. My face became hot as I quickly shook my head no and began to take the sign down.

Satisfied with her shaming, the director grinned, pivoted, and replied over her shoulder, "Be sure to seek *approval* the next time you want to redecorate this office space!"

The director and her guests laughed as they walked away, and I took the sign down. The message I received during this impressionable time in my career was:

▶ You do not have the authority, nor the permission, to set boundaries.

- You are expected to *always* be available.
- You need power and permission to set boundaries. And this permission, should you seek it, may not always be granted.

These heavy feelings weighed on me for a good portion of my internship. I would later reflect on how I learned to attach shame to boundary setting. I needed this reflection to make sure that in going forward, I *affirmed to myself* that I *deserve* to set boundaries and I do not deserve to be shamed for it.

One primary reason why it is difficult for many Black women to engage in self-care is because of the barriers we experience to set and maintain boundaries. These include:

- Not being supported in setting boundaries
- Being shamed or manipulated into not setting boundaries
- Not knowing when to set boundaries
- Feeling guilty for setting boundaries

Affirmation

I am capable of doing things I never thought I could do. My life proves it.

 **SELF-REFLECT**

Depending on where you are in your journey to take care of yourself better, you may have many reasons as to why you have trouble setting and maintaining boundaries. Recognizing what your limits and expectations are, creating space to establish them, and maintaining the boundaries you have worked so hard to bring about will require your attention, energy, and self-awareness. Reflect on your experiences with boundary setting below.

What do you think of when you think of setting and maintaining boundaries?

_____

_____

_____

_____

What were you taught about boundaries in your girl-hood? Were your personal boundaries encouraged or unsupported?

_____

_____

_____

_____

When was a time that you tried to set boundaries and it did not go well?

_____

_____

_____

_____

What would you want to tell your younger self now about setting boundaries? What does she need to hear?

_____

_____

_____

List three boundaries that come to mind when you think about your self-care in your adulthood.

1. _____

2. _____

3. _____

Who in your life is respectful of your boundaries? How do you know they are respectful?

_____

_____

_____

_____

Who in your life has difficulty respecting your boundaries? How does this make you feel?

_____

_____

_____

_____

Name one boundary that you are confidently able to maintain. What helps you maintain this boundary?

_____

_____

Think of one boundary that has been difficult for you to maintain lately. What makes it difficult to maintain this boundary?

_____

_____

When learning to set and maintain boundaries to take care of yourself better, consider mindfully removing the Black Superwoman cape from your shoulders. It's heavy and requires much of you to wear it day after day. What would it look like for you to put down your Black Superwoman cape, even if only temporarily? What would you need to take a break from all that you do?

_____

_____

_____

_____

———————— ❖ ————————

Affirmation

Today I will focus on what's important to me rather than what is urgent to others.

Ways to begin setting stronger boundaries:

▶ Practice saying no to small requests and mundane tasks.

▶ Recognize what your self-care needs are ahead of time so you're aware of what boundaries are needed to protect them.

▶ Honor your feelings, both heavy and light, instead of ignoring, denying, or minimizing them to "keep the peace."

- Know that, in some cases, you may need to restate and reinforce the boundaries that you put in place for them to be maintained.

- If you can, disconnect from people, as well as from places and spaces, that do not respect your boundaries.

 SELF-REFLECT

Choose one boundary to maintain around rest and putting down your cape. What is one way you can choose to not "do it all" this week?

List your intention for creating this boundary this week. What makes this intention important to you?

_____

_____

_____

_____

How do you want to maintain this boundary?

How would you know if someone or something was challenging this boundary?

Who or what can help you maintain this boundary?

Is there anything you can delegate, plan, or ask for help with to maintain this boundary?

_____

_____

_____

_____

————————— ❖ —————————

Affirmation

I can give myself permission to rest and recharge.

SELF CHECK-IN: PUTTING DOWN YOUR SUPERWOMAN CAPE

What did you learn about yourself in this section?

What are you in the process of unlearning?

What's your definition of boundary setting?

How would you like to take off your Black Superwoman cape?

_____

_____

_____

Which boundaries are the most important to you today?

_____

_____

_____

————— ❖ —————

CHAPTER 4

Your Rest Is Restorative

What's been getting in the way of you getting the rest you need?

This is a question I often ask busy, hardworking Black women. It's an important question, as there are usually responsibilities, behaviors, social constructions, and even mindset issues that get in the way of you getting the rest that you need (and deserve).

I often hear:

- "I don't have time. There's just too much on my plate."
- "I really feel bad when taking time out for me to rest."
- "I know I'm tired, but I'd rather push through it and just get this done."

Sound familiar?

Many of us struggle with getting the rest we need. Our schedules are packed, and our task lists overflowing. From parenting to working, to studying and adulting, instead of intentionally creating space for rest, a lot of times our bodies just shut down.

One of the most important reasons to make sure you have your rest is to avoid reaching the point of burnout. Burnout occurs when you're exhausted, disconnected, and have reached the breaking point of your working role, your caregiving role, or both. This feeling of burnout happens over a period of time and can occur in your professional role, in a parenting role, or in any role where you are taking care of others.

The last time I felt significant burnout was when I was working one full-time and two part-time jobs, at the same time. I was trying my best to earn my clinical social work license, with the hopes of opening my own therapy practice one day. I worked over fifty hours every week to fulfill my responsibilities and felt completely drained at the end of each workday. The weekends were never long enough, and my vacation time always felt too short. In an effort to do *all* things, I was burning out faster than I could imagine.

And at this stage in my career, I knew I was reaching my breaking point. Most of my waking hours were dedicated to working. I had trouble focusing and felt guilty when I was not working. I knew I needed to make a change, but I was terrified to decide what was best for me. I knew I couldn't go through another week working the hours that I did. I needed to figure out how in the world I would be able to create space for my rest. So I put a plan together to quit my full-time job.

Quitting jobs as a social worker has *never* been easy for me. I usually feel emotionally connected to the professional roles that I've held, and this particular job was *very* special to me. This job taught me so much as a social worker, and I was motivated to help fulfill the mission of the organization. In all honesty, I *loved* the work and was good at it. And, of course, the income was consistent and steady. What more could a girl ask for?

And sometimes that's the toughest part—for me, I had to recognize that just because I *could* do something did not mean I *had* to do it. I had to learn to reprioritize my rest and place my basic needs higher on the to-do list.

In choosing to quit this job, I was *intentionally* creating space for my rest to be a top priority. I crunched the numbers and did the math. I could financially afford to make this move and create the space I needed to improve my well-being. I had to muster the courage to leave this job that I cared so much about. With some thoughtful planning and the support of my therapist, I presented my letter of resignation and bravely moved forward with leaving my job, and the burnout that came with it, behind.

SELF-REFLECT

Creating space for your rest may require you to take some brave steps forward. You may need to plan for it, schedule it, ask for help, or make adjustments to make sure that you are not consistently reaching the point of exhaustion on a regular basis. Reflect on your experiences with burnout below.

Have you felt burned out lately? What does it look like when you're feeling burnout?

_____

_____

_____

_____

How do you know when you're feeling burnout? How do you know when your body is feeling burnout?

_____

_____

_____

_____

When was the last time you felt burnout? What did you do?

_____

_____

_____

What helps you prevent burnout?

_____

_____

_____

———————— ❖ ————————

Rest is a form of your resistance.

Similar to the historical trauma generations before us have experienced, many Black women have been denied the grace, time, and respect to rest our bodies. Instead, many Black women were historically punished for having the human need of rest.

Give yourself permission to unlearn that you do not deserve rest—you are entitled to the rest that you need. We need rest because we are exhausted from the physical, mental, and emotional experience of surviving as Black women. Acknowledging your need for rest is not a sign of weakness—it is human.

Making sure that you can receive the type of rest that restores you is essential for your self-care. There are many ways we, as Black women, can receive rest to cope with all that we have been exposed to. Rest can include intentional and voluntary moments of peace, as well as freedom from experiencing or witnessing traumatic events and interactions.

Affirmation

Choosing to let go of what's no longer valuable to me gives me space, energy, and time to focus on what is.

 **SELF-REFLECT**

We all have different ideas of what it means to get rest. For some of us, it's sleeping. For others, rest looks like taking an uninterrupted break from work or catching your breath when the kids are down for a nap. Let's take a look at what rest looks like for you.

Write or draw what your rest looks like below.

Describe your ideal ways to get some rest. You may have one way, or you may have several. Brainstorm your ideas here:

Do you have certain comforts, times of day, or rituals you like to include in your rest?

_____

_____

_____

If you had two weeks to yourself, how would you like to spend that time resting?

_____

_____

_____

If you had one hour to yourself, how would you like to spend that time resting?

_____

_____

_____

How do you know when you've gotten enough rest? How does your body tell you that you're well rested?

_____

_____

_____

Do you ever feel bad or guilty about choosing to rest? If so, how come?

_____

_____

_____

There may be a few reasons why you hesitate to listen to your body when you need rest from working, parenting, studying, or whatever else is on your plate right now. When was the last time you noticed you needed to rest and decided to push through instead?

_____

_____

_____

What are three ways you can recognize that you deserve to rest, without feeling bad about it?

_____

_____

_____

_____

—————— ❖ ——————

Preparing for rest:

▶ Create a routine before bed that helps you get the rest you need. These ideas can help aid your ability to sleep more soundly:

- Drink a warm drink, such as lavender or chamomile tea.
- Decrease your time spent on electronic devices before going to bed.
- Take a warm bath.
- Light a calming, scented candle.
- Rub on an essential oil.
- Listen to music that helps you relax.
- Participate in a guided meditation.
- Dim bright lights.
- Use blackout curtains to make your bedroom darker.
- Invest in a weighted blanket to help calm your body and decrease restlessness.

Alternative ways you can rest:

▶ Sit down and elevate your feet for five to ten minutes.
▶ Take a break from overstimulating content, such as social media or the news.

- Temporarily put your phone on a Do Not Disturb setting, turn off your social media and email notifications, or do both for a period of time.
- Take a nap.
- Tune into your body's needs with stretching, yoga, deep breathing, or all three.

Create three reminders to yourself as to why you *deserve* to create space for your self-care:

1. _____

2. _____

3. _____

———————— ❖ ————————

Affirmation

My glow is enhanced when I've had a chance to take care of myself.

SELF CHECK-IN: YOUR REST IS RESTORATIVE

What did you learn about yourself in this section?

_____

_____

_____

What are you in the process of unlearning about getting the rest you need?

_____

_____

_____

_____

What is your definition of "getting enough rest"?

What boundaries do you want to begin setting around your rest?

What is one way that you want to start prioritizing your rest better?

CHAPTER 5

Celebrating Who You Are

What does it mean to celebrate yourself? When we think of celebrating, we often think about:

▶ *Traditional celebrations*: celebrating a person or occasion annually, such as recognizing birthdays, holidays, or anniversaries

▶ *Achievement-based celebrations*: celebrating a person or group for accomplishing a goal, such as graduating, moving into a new home, or receiving a promotion at work

▶ *Celebrations for happy endings and new beginnings*: celebrating life's transitions, such as retirement, moving-away parties, farewell parties, marriage ceremonies

But there are many more ways to include celebration into your life that aren't centered around tradition or achievement. Why should you include celebrating *yourself* for self-care? Because you are worth celebrating! There's a good chance that you are doing wonderful, important, and incredible things that do not neatly fall into the categories listed above.

Celebrating yourself is far from a selfish act; celebrating yourself is a powerful way to show yourself love. Celebrating yourself includes praising and rewarding yourself without depending on others to do the celebrating for you. Celebrating yourself and your value is a special way to increase your feelings of self-pride and positive self-esteem.

For my twenty-fifth birthday, I decided to do something I had never done before. I decided to intentionally celebrate my birthday *alone*.

Every year, I always felt pressured to "celebrate" my birthday with others. From throwing a party to planning a trip, coordinating my birthday plans had a lot to do with *other* people. Unfortunately, over the years, sometimes planning my birthday began to feel less and less about *me*. I would regularly feel pressured to make sure everyone else had a good time and felt that everything was planned perfectly. More often than not, these birthdays would feel disappointing and stressful.

So when turning twenty-five, I decided to change it up. I didn't want to worry about anyone else but myself. I wanted to take an intentional break from caring for others. I didn't want to go through the stress of planning, and I wanted to do something I had never done before. So I booked a trip to Tucson, AZ, to spend my twenty-fifth year of life at a Southwestern spa and resort.

I remember my loved ones scratching their heads when they asked me what I was up to for my birthday.

"You *sure* you want to do that?" they asked me, eyebrows raised.

"*Absolutely*," I would reply confidently.

"Well, are you meeting anybody there?"

"Nope. It'll just be me."

This was a test for me to not overexplain my decision but to feel firm in it. It was OK if everyone didn't understand it. And little did I know that I was already forming my own birthday catchphrase.

From the security line to touching down on the quaint town that is Tucson, I was asked over and over again, "Just *you*?"

"Yep, just me."

From enjoying my lunch outside to heading to the spa, I was asked repeatedly, "Just *you*?"

"Yes, just me."

At one point, I turned the "just you" questions into a game with myself, giggling at how amazed folks were at seeing a young Black woman choosing to spend time with herself. I bought myself cupcakes, enjoyed some champagne, and made the most out of my time spent with "just me."

I remember how my nervous feelings of being alone began to melt away and feeling affirmed that I made the right decision. This space I had created for myself gave me so many opportunities to not worry about anyone *but* me. And this opportunity was a gift in itself. I fondly remember choosing to spend that birthday alone, to treat and spoil myself, and to not have any expectations for how the trip was "supposed" to be. To free myself of those social burdens was *liberating*. Celebrating myself, my way, was something I didn't even know I needed.

 SELF-REFLECT

With the many pressures that come with being a Black woman, it is important to recognize, honor, and celebrate your authentic self. Self-acceptance, self-celebration, and authenticity are all essential aspects of taking care of yourself well. Reflect on how you would like to celebrate your authentic self with the prompts below.

When was the last time you celebrated yourself?

_____

_____

_____

_____

What is your favorite way to celebrate yourself?

_____

_____

_____

_____

What is one way that you've wanted to treat yourself that
you have been wanting to do for a while?

_____

_____

_____

_____

If you had unlimited resources and time, how would you ideally like to celebrate yourself?

_____

_____

_____

_____

———————— ❖ ————————

Not sure _why_ you should celebrate yourself?

You should celebrate yourself because:

▶ You are growing and changing.

▶ You took a (big or small) step toward a goal.

▶ You set a boundary.

▶ You maintained a boundary.

▶ You were consistent.

▶ You kept a promise to yourself.

▶ You stepped outside your comfort zone.

▶ You chose to be courageous.

▶ You did something you've never done before.

▶ You felt proud of yourself.

Ideas to celebrate yourself:

- Purchase a gift for yourself off your wish list.
- Take yourself out on the town.
- Plan a vacation for yourself.
- Pat yourself on the back.
- Treat yourself to something special.
- Schedule a day off.
- Have a staycation.

Tips for celebrating yourself:

- Expand your views of "achievement" and reaching milestones.
- Recognize your value outside of what you do.
- Learn to appreciate the small goals you achieve and complete.

Affirmation

The amount of work that I do does not determine why I care for myself.
I do not have to earn my self-care.

ACTIVITY: LOVIN' ON ME

Set a timer for three minutes. In those three minutes, list as many things that you love about yourself as you can. There are no limits to what you love about yourself; write down everything that comes to mind below.

What did you notice about yourself with this activity?

_____

_____

_____

What felt easy and effortless about listing what you love about yourself?

_____

_____

What felt hard or challenging about listing what you love about yourself?

_____

_____

Without using a timer, reflect on the following prompts:

Which talents, skills, or strengths are you most proud of?

_____

_____

_____

Name one unique trait that you find special about yourself.

_____

What does self-love mean to you?

_____

_____

List three ways that you show yourself love:

1. _____

2. _____

3. _____

What is one part of you that is sometimes difficult to love?
Describe this part of you.

_____

_____

_____

What makes this part of you difficult to love?

_____

_____

What does this part of you need today?

_____

_____

———————— ❖ ————————

Affirmation

Celebrating myself isn't self-indulgent.
It is a powerful way that I show myself self-love.

Along with celebrating yourself, it is important to recognize your authentic self.

What do you think of when you think about your authentic self?

When I think about being my authentic self, I think about being the person I can be without thinking twice about it—the person who is free, without limits and without wearing a mask.

For so many Black women, being your authentic self feels like a privilege. In many spaces, our authentic selves are not welcomed and are not given permission to shine. Depending on the settings and the social expectations, many Black women feel safer wearing a "mask" to protect their authentic self from potential harm.

These social masks that we sometimes wear can look like a plethora of things, with code-switching being one of the most prevalent.

Code-switching is the act of engaging socially with others, usually non-White folx, and adhering to the "mainstream" ways of communicating, relating, and connecting. Code-switching often involves protecting your authentic self in these spaces, so you can adjust, adapt, and survive. Many Black women code-switch in settings where they are the minority, or feel like the minority, to get through the social experience. Code-switching, as well as other ways of protecting your authentic self, can be fatiguing. And depending on how often you feel the need to wear it, it can even be hard to take the mask off.

Code-switching was a normal part of my life as a young Black girl who moved around a lot. As a kid who moved to city after city for the first few years of my life, code-switching was a daily habit I wasn't even aware that I was using. Because of my father's profession, my family moved almost every year I was in elementary school. Like clockwork, we would pick up and move in the summers just in time for my brother and me to start the school year at a different school.

Many of the schools I attended were predominately White. I would often be the only Black girl in the class, and often I had my handy, code-switching mask in my back pocket to protect my authentic self. My norm was to nod and smile when asked about my hair texture and regularly explain that because my skin was dark, that didn't mean my eyes were "black" too. It became second nature for me to "switch" into this well-to-do Black girl who could blend in as well as she could in a White space.

The effect of putting on this mask so often, at a time when my identity was still developing, had the possibility of being damaging. As a little Black girl, I was learning that my authentic self could breathe only in safe spaces. And like many Black girls experiencing the same thing, I didn't have this process explained to me. I had no idea that I was taking steps to take care of myself.

Protecting your authentic self does not always have to result in code-switching, but it is important to recognize that many spaces are not designed to be safe for Black women. Know that it's OK for you to do what you need to do to protect yourself.

Affirmation

My self-compassion will take me places my self-criticism is afraid to go.

SELF-REFLECT

Have you felt the need to protect your authentic self? Reflect on your experiences with authenticity below.

Describe a time when your authentic self was able to shine. What happened during this event?

_____

_____

_____

In which spaces can you be your most authentic self? What about these spaces helps you feel comfortable enough to be your authentic self?

_____

_____

_____

How do you protect your authentic self?

_____

_____

_____

Do you feel you need to code-switch? When was the last time that you had to code-switch?

_____

_____

_____

Whom do you feel you do not have to "perform" for? Who sees you for you?

_____

_____

_____

Here are a few ideas on how to protect your authentic self:

▶ Give yourself permission to protect your authentic self when you need to.

▶ Set boundaries in spaces where you feel like you cannot be your authentic self.

▶ Spend time in your cultural community and with people who help you feel safe as a Black woman.

▶ Create space to enjoy your culture and your Blackness without having to explain or be questioned by non-Black folx.

▶ Engage in self-loving acts and practices.

▶ Treat yourself with kindness.

▶ Take care of your basic needs.

Write a letter to your future self. What do you want your future self to know? What do you think she'll need to hear from you?

_____

_____

_____

_____

_____

_____

_____

_____

_____

_____

_____

_____

SELF CHECK-IN: CELEBRATING WHO YOU ARE

What did you learn about yourself in this section?

_____

_____

_____

What are you in the process of unlearning?

_____

_____

_____

How do you want to celebrate yourself?

_____

_____

_____

Do you feel the need to protect your authentic self? If so, how would you like to protect it?

_____

_____

_____

_____

What's your favorite way to practice self-love?

_____

_____

_____

_____

CHAPTER 6

Reclaiming Your Culture

Healing can come with reclaiming our culture and what is important to us.

Liberation from racial- and gender-based trauma is celebrating the joy of being a Black woman. Connecting to, having pride in, and reclaiming our culture is self-care and community care. It is how we can take care of ourselves and take pride in who we are as Black women.

So many of the injustices that we experience are caused and perpetuated by people benefiting from and causing oppression. Many aspects of our culture were purposefully exchanged for mainstream White culture, with the focus on assimilating Black people and appropriating Black culture. Reclaiming our culture helps us unlearn that we are unworthy of feeling happiness, safety, and freedom.

One of the most significant moments when I remember feeling an incredible sense of pride was during the 2008 presidential election: I voted for the first time as a US citizen, casting my vote for the man who would become the first Black president.

At the ripe old age of eighteen, I proudly stood in line to put my vote in for the Democratic candidate, Barack Obama. That night, I hosted myself and the girls on my college dorm floor. We kept our eyes glued to the news, waiting for the results to come in. When the final Electoral College numbers came in and Obama was declared the winner and my president for the next four years, I literally jumped for joy.

For me and for many other Black people, this moment was monumental. To have a president who looked like my family, a first lady who looked like me, and first children who resembled my relatives—it was a proud moment for our culture. President Obama's election and eventual reelection by no means solved all the issues regarding systemic oppression, but for Black folx who have lived year after year, election after election with White, male candidates, this moment in history was unlike any other.

Historical moments, like the 2008, 2012, and, eventually, the 2020 United States presidential election of the first Black, South Asian, and female vice president, are important parts of Black culture. Our culture has historically been filled with strife and injustice, as well as creativity, inspiration, art, and family. Reclaiming your culture is a special way to take care of yourself and feel pride in who you are.

 SELF-REFLECT

Which moments in history are significant to you in reclaiming your culture? Reflect on the historic moments you have lived through below.

What is a historical moment that you have lived through? What do you remember from this moment?

_____

_____

_____

_____

How do you feel witnessing and being a part of this historical moment?

_____

_____

_____

_____

What is one historical moment that is special in regard to reclaiming your culture?

―――――――――― ❖ ――――――――――

Allow reclaiming your culture to be a part of your self-care.

One of the best parts about reclaiming your culture is that *you* get to decide what that means for you. Reclaiming your culture can be any way you choose to embrace and rejoice in the practices, traditions, rituals, and events that honor and uplift your cultural identity.

There are many ways to view culture. There's our culture as a community of Black people—our references and history, our jokes, and our customs that are familiar to us as a people.

Then there's your personal culture—the culture you have from your unique and individual experience as a Black woman that's personal to you.

Similarly, you have a culture within your immediate family, your extended family, and the family you create, as well as within your own groups of loved ones, colleagues, and communities you live in. There is a good chance that you are a part of *many* cultures.

Enjoying and celebrating my own culture became a significant part of how I take care of myself. It is essential for me to be in safe spaces where my culture is more than tolerated—it is essential for me to be in spaces where my culture is loved, respected, and appreciated. For me, reclaiming my culture means relishing within my culture, completely guilt free.

Dance has always been one of my favorite ways to engage in my culture. Throughout my life, I loved to move to my favorite R&B, hip-hop, and soul music. I loved allowing the rhythm of the music to connect with my body and moving to the sounds that blasted from the speakers. Dance was a way that I would celebrate who I am and a major way that my loved ones could enjoy sharing space together. I would choreograph 3LW and Destiny's Child dances with girlfriends and try to hit the Bikers Shuffle and the Cha Cha Slide with my cousins. We loved to dance *our* way to our music.

As I got older and more secure with my authentic self, I started setting boundaries around teaching the White girls around me "how to twerk" and explaining rap lyrics. I found that reclaiming my culture also meant choosing when and what I wanted to give my energy to. To me, that part of a White person's privilege was to do their *own* research on *my* culture if they wanted to learn more about it. I learned that it was not my responsibility to teach them about Black culture. It was not my responsibility to fulfill their requests on "how to be Black."

Reclaiming your culture could look like both embracing the parts of your culture that are important to you and setting boundaries around protecting your culture. Again, you get to decide what reclaiming your culture looks like for you. The decision is 100 percent yours.

Affirmation

I will do what I need to do to take care of myself, as often as I can.

Here are a few ideas on how you can reclaim and celebrate your culture:

- Cooking a traditional meal
- Singing and dancing
- Laughing, telling jokes
- Sharing stories, oral history
- Practicing family rituals and traditions

- Joining culturally specific clubs, Greek-letter organizations, and advocacy groups
- Enjoying and creating artwork
- Showing honor to your elders and ancestors
- Watching or listening to our comedy shows
- Connecting to your spirituality, faith, and religion
- Watching Black movies, musicals, shows, and documentaries
- Supporting and promoting Black businesses

Affirmation

Today is another opportunity for me to put energy into what matters to me first.

SELF CHECK-IN: RECLAIMING YOUR CULTURE

What did you learn about yourself in this section?

What are you in the process of unlearning about reclaiming your culture?

What's one of your favorite parts of your culture?

How do you want to reclaim your culture?

What parts of your culture do you want to protect?

❖

CHAPTER 7

The Beauty of Black Womanhood

There are many sensational parts that come with being a Black woman. Our spirits, our bodies, our energy, and our culture are all incredible aspects of Black Womanhood. Being a Black woman is an exceptional experience. The intersection of Blackness and womanhood and all the intricacies in between make the experience of being a Black woman one that is unlike any other.

One of my most significant memories of embracing my Black Womanhood was when I was inducted into my sorority as an undergraduate college student.

Alpha Kappa Alpha Sorority, Incorporated (AKA), served as an incredible sisterhood for me to learn about Black Womanhood. Growing up, my mother, my aunts, and many of my cousins all pledged to become women in service to all mankind as members of the first Black sorority.

As a little girl I was my mother's shadow, following her to community service event after community service event, in full awe of the sea of women in pink and green who would be advocating for and helping take care of others. I remember watching with big eyes the classic parades and secretly wishing that I could grow up to be as elegant, sophisticated, and beautiful as the women of this sisterhood. Of the many dreams I had as a little girl, one of the most special was to one day become a member of AKA.

Fortunately, my dream came true. In the spring of 2009, I was honored to become a member of this prestigious sisterhood. And I did so at a crucial time in my early adulthood.

I attended one of the biggest, predominately White universities in Indiana, with over 40,000 students, and I shared academic and social space on this Midwestern campus. I had attended a high school that was *also* predominately White, and it was becoming my norm to not only statistically be the minority but to also *literally* be a minority everywhere I went. My first friends in college were well-intentioned White women from my dorm room and I was around many White peers. Everywhere I looked, I was the token Black girl. Part of my Black Womanhood experience was becoming aware of when my Blackness and my womanhood stood out. Though not intentionally, I felt like an outsider. I felt and looked different from my White peers. And I felt pressured to conform to my White peers' ways of living and being.

When I learned that I had a chance to join the sisterhood that I admired my entire life, I *jumped* at the opportunity. Because within this sorority, I had another experience of feeling *seen*. There was a cultural comfort and an enriching reassurance that I felt being in such close company of other Black women who shared my values and looked like me. Other than being in my own family, I hadn't felt *this* much at home.

From the older members who brought me into the sisterhood to my line sisters who were my peers, I was surrounded by Black Womanhood and elated by the members' acceptance of me. As a young member of this sorority, I felt empowered within my race and within my gender. I *finally* felt like I belonged. And this feeling changed my entire social life. From then on, I found solace in my place in this sorority and felt empowered as a Black woman.

 SELF-REFLECT

There may be many thoughts and feelings that come up for you when you think about your experience as a Black woman. Some of these thoughts may be light and joyful, while others may be heavy and sad. *All* of your thoughts are welcome here, as we recognize the complexities of being a Black woman in this day and age. Let's spend some time recognizing your feelings and thoughts about your experience as a Black woman.

Write down the first three things that come to mind when you think about being a Black woman.

1. _____

_____

2. _____

_____

3. _____

_____

What do you love about being a Black woman? What gives you joy about being a Black woman?

_____

_____

_____

_____

What feels challenging, stressful, or difficult about being a Black woman? What feels heavy about being a Black woman?

_____

_____

_____

_____

❖

Affirmation

I can grow through what I never thought I could go through.

Just as we recognize the beauty of Black Womanhood, we also recognize the difficulties of our experience. A variety of injustices are put in front of us to cope with on a regular basis—racism, discrimination, prejudice, inequality, and colorism, just to name a few. Our experiences of injustice are beyond challenging, are significantly exhausting, and have a substantial impact on how we can live our lives.

Collectively, Black people have experienced, have been exposed to, have witnessed, and have been victimized by heinous and violent injustices that have violated our safety, our rights, and our well-being. The traumatic fatigue of surviving and grieving about these experiences has a serious and devastating impact on Black people *everywhere*.

Many Black women have experienced a history of being treated inhumanely. This mistreatment has been a barrier for many of us to express our thoughts, feelings, and opinions without consequences or punishment. The inhumane treatment of Black people cannot be rationalized away, and many of us harbor complicated feelings about how racism and systemic oppression are repeatedly forced into our daily existence.

When I provided trainings for a nonprofit organization, I have a clear memory of feeling invisible as a Black woman. I was providing a training in southern rural Georgia for a group of advocates. This group was mostly White women, with two Black women present. The group described themselves as close knit as a staff.

The training I was facilitating with my coworkers was centered around equality and cultural humility in the nonprofit workplace. This training covered topics on recognizing racial bias, White fragility, and systemic oppression when providing services. There was no surprise that these topics brought up *a lot* of feelings in the training participants.

During a break, one of the participants asked to speak with me one on one. She was a White woman, born and raised in southern Georgia, and was in her early seventies. During the training, she asked about "not seeing color" and seeing all people as "equal" because of that. I quietly gulped as she approached me, knowing that this was going to be one of *those* conversations.

She placed her hand on my shoulder and self-confidently said, "I hope you weren't offended by what I said! I really don't see color! You could be black, blue, purple, or orange, and it wouldn't matter! You're beautiful anyway!" She smiled and raised her eyebrows, pleased with her own comments.

I felt my cheeks get warm and my throat become dry. I *knew* this was coming, but even in my professional work of helping end racism, these comments still have a sting to them. Because in all her self-satisfaction of attempting to console me, her comments were *still* racist.

To approach a Black woman at work and say her color doesn't matter *is racist.* This statement is a microaggression that indicates that I am invisible, that my people are invisible.

My color matters. I *am* Black. And to say you don't see that means that you don't see . . . me.

With the pressure of "being professional" looming over my head, I told this woman just that, that to say color doesn't matter is saying she doesn't see me. Like clockwork, her White fragility stepped in, and she became defensive in attempting to explain away her perspective, instead of listening to what I was saying. I worked in an organization with White women who were aspiring allies to Black people and, fortunately, we tried to create protocols around these interactions. I politely excused myself from her to tap in my White coworker. The emotional labor of going back and forth with this woman was just not something I wanted to do.

Know that it makes sense if you too feel exhausted when you are asked to talk about, explain, or process your experiences of racism with people outside the Black community. It can also feel draining to discuss racism with other Black people whose values do not align with your own.

This fatigue that you may feel is often called *emotional labor*. Emotional labor includes being asked to discuss, explain, provide details, or educate others about experiences of racism. Being asked or expected to explain your experiences of racism can feel like explaining a traumatic event over and over again. Emotional labor can also include repeated exposure to racial injustice from law enforcement, the criminal justice system, the health-care system, and other major systems that have power and control in our society today.

SELF-REFLECT

What is your take on emotional labor?

_____

_____

_____

_____

Has racism impacted you in a professional setting? If so, what happened?

_____

_____

_____

_____

When was the last time you experienced a microaggression? How did you know it was a microaggression?

Do you feel pressured to code-switch in professional settings?

I Own My Magic

What is one way you want to affirm your racial identity today?

_____

_____

_____

_____

❖

Because of our history, it makes sense if you sometimes feel limited, guilty, and ashamed to freely express yourself. Part of your self-care may be to gently learn that you deserve to express yourself freely, with no consequences or punishments.

In unlearning these deeply engrained thoughts, let's recognize and name what could be getting in the way of you expressing yourself today. Place a checkmark next to the statements that resonate with you the most.

In expressing how I feel as a Black woman, I have:

◗ Not been believed about my experience of racism

◗ Been blamed for experiencing, being exposed to, and being victimized by racism

- Witnessed other Black people experiencing, being exposed to, and being victimized by racism
- Felt drained and exhausted from the emotional labor of interacting with non-Black people
- Had to engage in code-switching
- Experienced and witnessed performative and casual activism by non-White people
- Been supervised and surveyed by non-Black people while engaging in daily activities
- Been stereotyped and discriminated against because of my race
- Felt pressured to educate non-Black people on my experience of racism, even when I did not want to

Just as you have the right to speak up about the racial injustices that affect you, also recognize that you have the right to reject, pause, and decline to talk about your experiences. Here are a few ways you can set this boundary:

- "No, I do not want to talk about what I've experienced at this time."
- "I am not in a place to discuss that with you."
- "No, I do not have the capacity to go into depth on that topic now."
- "NO."

I Own My Magic

Affirmation

Today, I will release what is holding me emotionally hostage.

How do you feel about your womanhood? Who inspires your Black Womanhood?

The Black woman who laid the groundwork for me to become the woman I am today is my mother, Gennifer.

My mother is a Southern woman to her core, born and raised in Carthage, MS. She has a generous heart and an infectious spirit that instantly lights up a room the minute she arrives. From her laugh, her smile, her grace, and her humility, my mother taught me how to be a giving woman and to care about others.

My mother has a *tremendous* impact on the people around her. I can't count how many times others would tell me how much they loved her, how special she made them feel, and how kind she was to them. I learned from her how to be a gracious hostess and how to take care of my own family. When I was a little girl, she fiercely protected me and my brother from anything that even *resembled* harm with her firm rules and guidelines. We groaned at the time, but my brother and I were blessed with the sacred opportunity to *really* be kids and under her parenting. Every day, she prioritized our needs to ensure that we were loved, healthy, and valued.

There was rarely a time when my mom didn't have my back. From tap dancing to cheerleading, and from preschool to graduate school, my mother was always there, supporting me, picking me up and encouraging me to do what I loved to do.

Being named after her, I took great pride in being compared to my mom.

"There goes little Gennifer!"

"Ooo, girl! You look just like your mama!"

"Are y'all sisters? Who's older?"

It was, and is, an honor to be compared to my beautiful mama. Not only in looks, but in character. She radiates Black beauty, on the inside and out. How special it is to be Gennifer's daughter.

 SELF-REFLECT

Reflect on your experiences as a Black girl, a younger Black woman, and the Black woman you are today. From girlhood to adolescence and from your earliest experiences of adulthood to where you are today, create space to honor who you have become and what you have overcome. Reflect on who supported you, cared for you, and loved you across your life span. Take a moment to think about the Black women in your life who lent a hand in helping you become the person you are today.

Think of one Black woman from your girlhood who inspired you. What about her inspired you?

Name one Black woman from your adolescent years whom you admired. What did you admire about her?

Who is the Black woman whom you feel most connected to today? Describe your connection to her.

What feels joyful about being a Black woman today? What feels difficult?

Who uplifts your Black Womanhood? Who positively supports who you are as a Black woman?

Affirmation

Each step I take toward taking care of myself, no matter how big or small, is a necessary step for me to feel whole.

Gender discrimination, inequalities, and violence based on our gender have their own impact on the experience of a Black woman. Black women are stereotyped as angry, over-sexualized, or completely devoid of sexuality as maternal figures. These views of Black Womanhood are limiting, continue to deny our humanness, and can interrupt our sense of safety.

These stereotypes, moments, and experiences are sometimes minimized, denied, or ignored by others. As part of your experience as a Black woman, you may have survived difficult, uncomfortable, and harmful experiences. Many Black women feel unprotected and vulnerable when our safety is compromised or in jeopardy. Here, we want to hold space for the moments and times when you did not always feel safe, physically, emotionally, and spiritually.

SELF-REFLECT

With this section, please take your time and explore each question at your own discretion. Consider connecting with someone you trust to process what comes up for you, if needed.

As a Black woman, what does it mean for you to feel safe? In which spaces do you feel the safest?

_____

_____

_____

_____

Which spaces in your life and in your environment feel less safe for you? What about these spaces feels less safe for you?

_____

_____

_____

_____

What did you need during the moments in your life when you did not feel safe?

_____

_____

_____

_____

What helps you feel safe today? What about your safety do you feel you have control over?

_____

_____

_____

_____

Write a letter to your younger self, a young Black girl. What would you want your younger self to know? What did she need to hear?

_____

_____

_____

_____

_____

_____

_____

_____

_____

_____

_____

—————— ❖ ——————

ACTIVITY: FEELING SAFE

Take a moment to freely brainstorm or draw words, thoughts, affirmations, and messages that help you feel safe. Refer back to this exercise and add to it with as many images and words as you would like.

Affirmation

I do not have to shift to put others ahead
of myself or my needs. I am allowed to
take up as much space as I want.

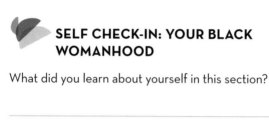

SELF CHECK-IN: YOUR BLACK WOMANHOOD

What did you learn about yourself in this section?

_____

_____

_____

What are you in the process of unlearning about your
Black Womanhood?

_____

_____

_____

What is your favorite reflection about being a Black woman?

_____

_____

_____

_____

From what you've reflected, how do you want to take care of your Black Womanhood?

_____

_____

_____

_____

Name one practice you want to put energy into to take care of your Black Womanhood in the future.

_____

_____

_____

_____

———————— ❖ ————————

Closing

What did you learn about yourself after self-reflecting with this journal?

_____

_____

_____

_____

You explored so many parts of who you are, what you need to take care of yourself, and what is important to you, that you may have many feelings coming up for you as you reach the end of this journal.

From caring for your health to releasing your Black Superwoman cape, to celebrating your Black Womanhood, to reclaiming your culture, it is important for you to recognize the incredible Black woman that you are and all you have done to reach this point in your life.

Take the self-discoveries that you have learned in this journal and begin to apply them to your daily life. Review the journal entries that you completed to take care of yourself better.

Set up a routine or a sacred time to continue to self-reflect and pour into yourself. Allow your self-care to become a regular part of your life.

You are so deserving of your own care and love. I hope that in taking the time to reflect on who you are, what you have survived, and what you deserve, you were able to create space to *own your magic*.

Affirmation

Today, I will chart the path to own. my. magic.

Suggested Reading

Brown, Brene. *The Gifts of Imperfection: Let Go of Who You Think You're Supposed to Be and Embrace Who You Are*. Center City, MN: Hazelden Publishing, 2010.

Burke, Tarana. *Unbound: My Story of Liberation and the Birth of the Me Too Movement*. New York: Flatiron Books, 2021.

Burke, Tarana, and Brene Brown. *You Are Your Best Thing*: Vulnerability, Shame Resilience, and the Black Experience. New York: Random House, 2021.

Burton, Valorie. *Let Go of the Guilt*. Nashville, TN: W Publishing, 2020.

Cooper, Brittany. *Eloquent Rage: A Black Feminist Discovers Her Superpower*. New York: St. Martin's Press, 2018.

DeGruy, Joy A. *Post Traumatic Slave Syndrome: America's Legacy of Enduring Injury and Healing*. Portland, OR: Joy DeGruy Publications Inc, 2017.

Delia, Lalah, *Vibrate Higher Daily: Live Your Power*. San Francisco: HarperOne, 2019.

Elle, Alex. *After the Rain: Gentle Reminders for Healing, Courage, and Self-Love*. San Francisco: Chronicle Books, 2020.

Glover Tawwab, Nedra. *Set Boundaries, Find Peace*: A Guide to Reclaiming Yourself. New York: TarcherPerigee, 2021.

Goodloe, Michelle. *The Self-Care Investment: Your Guide to Making Your Self-Care Non-Negotiable*. New York: Barnes & Noble Press, 2021.

Jones, Luvvie Ajayi. *Professional Troublemaker: The Fear-Fighting Manual*. New York: Penguin Life, 2021.

Kendall, Mikki. *Hood Feminism: Notes from the Women That a Movement Forgot*. New York: Viking Press, 2020.

Menakem, Resmaa. *My Grandmother's Hands: Racialized Trauma and the Pathway to Mending Our Hearts and Bodies*. Las Vegas: Central Recovery Press, 2017.

Taylor, Sonya Renee. *The Body Is Not an Apology: The Power of Radical Self-Love*. San Francisco: Berrett-Koehler Publishers, 2018.

Winters, Mary-Frances. *Black Fatigue: How Racism Erodes the Mind, Body, and Spirit*. Oakland, CA: Berrett-Koehler Publisher, 2020.

About the Author

G. Michelle Goodloe is a licensed clinical social worker and an experienced project manager dedicated to helping others develop healthy relationships with themselves and with others.

With a professional background in providing clinical interventions, compassion-based services, and statewide advocacy for people impacted by domestic violence, child abuse, and stress-related conflict, the focus of Michelle's career has been to develop and institute accessible and resourceful avenues of support through her agencies: The Essence of Healing LLC and gmichelle.com.

Michelle is the owner and psychotherapist with The Essence of Healing LLC, a private therapeutic practice based in Atlanta, GA. The Essence of Healing LLC provides individual and couples psychotherapy to adult residents in the states of Georgia and Illinois.

She is also the creator of the wellness-resource website, gmichelle.com. Gmichelle.com offers busy, caring people the opportunity to make self-care a practical part of their lives. Michelle facilitates interactive workshops for nonprofit and private organizations that experience challenges with addressing self-care, compassion fatigue, and professional burnout.